I0170518

Life, Love, Family and Friends:
Poems

I closed my eyes and listened

Gordon Emmerson

Copyright Gordon Emmerson 2016
Old Golden Point Press
Blackwood, Victoria: Australia

ISBN: 10: 0-9924995-4-2
ISBN: 13: 978-0-9924995-4-9

Introduction

This book contains a selection of poems that I wrote through the years, from my early twenties. It was a difficult decision for me to put them out. That decision was made based on the feeling that they were gifts to me from where-ever poems come, so it is right that they be shared.

When I looked at the poems they appeared to belong in five groups, so the chapters are organized that way. I hope they speak to some of you, as they have spoken to me.

Life & Living

Relationships

Writing

Dreams & Fantasies

Friends & Family

Contents

1 Life and Living

1.1 The Roughened Shell

In life, I touched a shell so large,
With points so rough, and skin so hard,
My touch was pain and plain disgust,
That such a thing was here to touch.

My wish was not to see that shell,
And never feel its pain again,
To keep myself away from where it was,
Or where it ever might have been.

Yet, there it stood, in front of me,
Rough, ugly, sharp and grey.
How dare that cutting, hurting thing,
Come back and be that way.

My hate was peaked.
My fear was marked.
My action un-withstrained.
And what my action was,
Was more than I had dreamed.

Strike once, and twice,
My words came down,
With might upon the shell.

But, what I saw beneath the rough,
I shudder, yet, to tell.

Inside that thing, I hated such,
That destruction filled my mind,
Lay smooth and fragile tinted parts,
Of an awe, and wonder kind.

And when I see the roughened shell,
Upon the beach of life,
I think of how beneath the rough,
There lies a beauty shrine.

1.2   A Forgotten Tree

The field I cross a hundred times I've crossed before,

and I think on this trip more,

of the stately tree

than err within a trip I've crossed before.

It is a tree of majesty,

but, though I've seen it a hundred times before,

my notice now would not be here,

and my walk would be on down the hill,

if, in some manner, it were gone from where it's always stood.

It's sad to think of such a tree

with arms of strength and stately dignity,

not leaving one who has crossed its field as many times as I,

with memories strong enough to make me wonder why,

if it were gone from where it's always stood.

Yet, in my mind I know this tree,

and know its strength

and know its dignity,

for while I've crossed this field a hundred times before,

there is a thing it's given me.

Each time I've walked along this place
and gazed across the field,
this tree has slipped inside myself,
while I was thinking something else,
and stayed with me,
and gave a lending of its dignity.

So,
this tree is mine,
and even as I pass, if it were gone,
and if I, or no one knew,
it would not die, not in me, or not in other passers-by.

1.3   Touching and Creating

Everything we touch is partly our creation.
A child is raised and our interaction with that child deposits
self upon the earth, and that endures when self is gone.

A conversation leaves the listener changed,
and that change is a living creation.

A smile or frown reflects throughout eternity,
and that in itself is a great responsibility.

The change to the physical, in paint, in the forest or on the
table leaves new scenes and they are part of our creation.

As we exist we create, and what we create is left to reflect us,
who we are, and who we were.
We touch a person, animal, place, or thing and with our touch
we leave them changed.
This is our legacy and our waves live forever.

1.4 Fly Ride the Storm

Fly ride the melodic storm of life.

Feel the forceful winds and be proud of them,
for they are mutual to all who rise to see the flash of light.

Choose stay above the cellar,
weathering the thunders of those who doubt.

Feel fear and woe and glad and glow,
for in these you have your freedom.

Fly ride the storm and fill you up
with winds that blow and bide you.

Your wings will grow and you may know
no place to hide inside you.

1.5 My Tomorrow

Tomorrow I will be standing in a place I have not seen before, surrounded by people I have not met.

How I touch that place and those people,
and how they touch me will be determined by my thoughts and actions tomorrow.

My life will be new and my possibilities limited only by how I used my yesterdays.
I cannot change my yesterdays, but I can add to those I have, others of better quality.

I can add today, then my next tomorrow will be less limited.
It is my job today to determine what my past needs so I can have a better future.

1.6   The Eagle

Praise well the eagle through the skies, who flaps its wings and climbs to heights not known to it before.

Praise well the one who dares to fly
to reach the limits of the sky,

Praise well the one who makes its way above uncertainties
that prey upon the foul who flap their wings too low,

Praise well the eagle through the skies,
who aims the ways its wings will fly.

Praise well the one who knows.

1.7   Clocks and Cords

Damn you clock!

What gives you the power to tell me what to do?

There you sit, humming away, with not even a brain, hurling demands.

It wouldn't matter to you if I did jerk your plug
or smash your vulgar little body into a thousand pieces.

You would just lie there, overpoweringly saying,
"Now how are you going to know when to leave?"

Damn you clock!

You don't even do your own punishing.

You tell me when to move, when to jump, when to get excited.

But if I don't, if I stick up my nose just once and say, "No!
No, I'm not your puppet," your cronies make accommodations.

My job, my appointment, where have I been?

I'm yelled at, because I didn't listen to your ugly, little, expressionless face.

You hold the strings.
You have it made, just sitting there.

And the sad part is, the power isn't even coming down that crooked little cord.

1.8 Wildfire

The talk is hot of that wretched Jones lot,
and all the nasty, sinful things they do.

Did you know that, and she's so fat,
and he can't know what she's up to.

The word's around, it's all over town.
Oh, I can't believe, but it has to be true.

Well, I … do tell!,
Why, she'll go to …
Well, I guess that's nothing really new.

You've made my day.
They should lock her away.
I wonder if he knows what he's been through?

Thanks for the tip.
I won't let it slip.
You know me, just as I know you.

1.9 Glimpses

On the hill.

What is that?

The path I travel is one of time.

It's always moving.

Hard to see.

Far away, on the hill, light silhouettes a figure.

Too far to hear, but still unmistakable.

Like in another world, yet in mine.

The air wrinkles, and there is nothing.

Doubt comes quickly,

like a wave on the beach,

to wash away what was written on my mind.

Then, there it is,

far away, and clear.

And now, I will remember.

1.10 Beyond Thought

The hills and mountains and sky, they try to hold me.
They can't. My spirit extends them.
The earth acts well as a prison keeper,
and the star that sits above my head sings a sweet and
tempting song, but I am not swayed.

I look above the earth, and beyond the star,
and not with my eyes.
I travel without speed or time, and without myself.
Beyond thought, I am no longer separate,
but part of all, knowing and existing.

1.11 A silent space

Beyond the moon is a silent space,
where exists no mountains
and exists no lakes.

There are no cautions
and nothing required.
There is no time
and there is no place.

There is only knowing
for knowing's sake.

It is from this knowing that we have come,
to learn asleep what we cannot awake.

It is to this knowing that we shall return,
to know again for knowing's sake.

1.12 The Gift

I've landed in a gift for which I have long waited.

The ride I have chosen needs well to be ridden.

Yes, I could see the end, but could not feel the middle.

Could I have, why would I have come?

I can see now part of what I have ridden and I hope to ride better.

My intent is to gain the wisdom and have the courage.

I am blessed, as are we all.

1.13 I Stepped into Life

Without recalling the reason why, I stepped into a cave.
Who and where I was, was a mystery I did not question.
The dark cave lightened as my eyes adjusted, revealing separate paths to all directions.

Which one to take, or should I stay where I stood?
The wrong path could lose me and my room was possibly better than any other.

My room moved from itself into my head, although it still surrounded me.
I moved through a passage in a wall hunting other rooms,
but even if I lose my way there is always one room in my mind.

Rooms are everywhere I go, some good, and some not so,
All different, yet just the same.
In each I leave my little echo.

There are holes in which to fall, and mountains here to climb,
but for neither do I spend much time, for there are other rooms to find.

I cannot remember before the cave, and I'm not ready yet to go.

I will probably choose a room and spend my time shining one of its walls, hoping the reflection I leave will guide others and not blind them,
Both while I am here and when I am gone.

1.14 Life's Feast

Wide or narrow, we need correction
while moving down the steady stream.

That stream's walls are slick and scarred with scratches,
showing vain attempts at pauses
in life's ever flowing current,
from which escape comes only in a dream.

Our work is left behind as time moves us along.

We will feast upon the work we've left
once we've floated through the mouth,
and as we walk back along the banks,
with ever flowing time between the walls below,
an ecstasy we'll feel, if our hunger does not grow.

2 Relationships

2.1 Music by my Maiden

T'was once I knew a maiden fair
who walked with high step
among those trees,
just down the lane.

The smile she gave
was both once innocent and alluring.

Many days I watched,
wishing her stop
where I, myself, was standing.

A call,
I thought,
might frighten her away.

So, each evening she passed,
carrying her beauty through the still light,
stepping high and reflecting my gaze
with a smile so faint
I wondered from where it came.

With innocence
and without knowing,
she brought to the forest,
life.

We belonged to her,
longed for her,
and her strides.

And the trees grew,
no less than I,
thankful for her claims.

Both,
thankful for her claims.

2.2 Life Beside Me

Long encouraged false traditions
Planted in the age of time,
Sprout confusion and emotion
As our separate paths entwine.

Even though our pasts do differ
And your present thoughts aren't mine,
What we have when we're together
Is too much to be confined.

These who want us going places
Other than the ones we choose
Cannot know the things within us,
all of what we have to lose.

I don't care of what they tell me,
Not of what I should not do,
What I want is life beside me,
And life I have when I'm with you.

2.3 Words

It came from her,
Accented by the slight stammer that proved the weight
of what she had to say.

Before a word…
Before a translation could be shoved into that dismal excuse
for communicating,

I knew.
I knew better than she could ever explain.
The air was full of it.
It filled me, and the room,
And stopped time, still.

Yet, she spoke.
What crude instruments.
What a useless ritual, in a time of such damnable clarity.

Like throwing nails at an already seething sore.
Like pouring water on a drowning man.
Like what she did, when she turned the other way.

2.4   When Time has come for Us to Part: Being Left

Time, why must you tell the one why you have come, but not the other?

All life is when we are us, and longing to be is all there is when we are parted.

My head cannot compete with what I feel, and what I say is not to help the parting.

To walk away and hold myself is not a thing that I could do, not when all I have is what I have to lose.

Please go away and never come, not for why you came.
Come for anything, but never come to part us.

Oh, Time, how can it be that you could be so cruel,
To tell the one but not to tell the other.

2.5 When Time has come for Us to Part: Leaving

Time, why must you tell the one why you have come, but not the other?

I want the end, the end I have to make, but, oh it hurts for me to hurt another.

To see the care and see what I must do gives me some of the pain the other's going through.

When you have come, there is no other way.
It's not a choice I have a choice to make.

Please tell us both what you told me, so both will know, and both will have my feeling.

Oh, Time, how can it be that you could be so cruel,
To tell the one but not to tell the other.

2.6 Listen

It is not with passion I call your name,

For passion is gone.

I have not seen Camelot and I no longer seek,

For my road has been long and hard.

You may see me in a state you may not want,

and if I am sent away the fault would be mine.

When you asked my stay, I left.

When you waited, I did not return.

Now,

much time has passed,

and I offer nothing but a used heart that has looked elsewhere

in vain.

It is your power, but do not turn me away to hurt,

For I already hurt.

Do not reject, if you want me.

For although I offer little, I want to stay.

I offer what is left.

It is less than you deserve,

But somewhere in your heart may remain a bit of your care.

If this is gone, and I am only what you see,

I will no longer bother.

I'll be on my way.

2.7   Love behind my Doors

While my doors are opened wide
Inside, with love, my fear resides.

For pain stays, too, behind those doors,
And though your love is well received,
Belief in it is hard for me.

My doors are flanked by doubt and trust,
My friends who can't agree.

Doubt will thrust both doors shut,
While Trust will fling them free.

With Doubt, I'm held from pain,
And too from what I need.
With Trust, I'm fragile frail,
But feeling fills my needs.

My doubt and trust, my friends who don't agree.

2.8 Us

Across a moon, a sun, a wall, a room, a day.

Across the words I speak, to the words I want to say.

Across the constant fear, there may not be a way.

Somewhere there lies the hope I have in me,

That you and I could somehow, someplace be.

2.9 Confused

Since your feelings may not match mine, I expect nothing.

Since my feelings may change, I promise nothing.

Since my feelings are real, I hope for something.

Since my feelings are confused, I do not know what.

2.10 Karma

The flow of music fills the air.
The one you like is standing there.

A touch of wind has tipped the trees.
The smell of spring is in the leaves.

A smile so faint it's barely seen,
Tells of the love there is between.

Reflection of a distant wing,
Takes up its place in everything.

The sun peeks through a floating cloud,
To touch the words I speak aloud.

"It's not a thing I often say,
But love is what I feel today."

2.11 A Thousand Years

A thousand years from now what I have done,
and what I do, will long have been forgotten.

The words I speak and paths I walk,
will long be changed by thousands others' tongues and feet.

And even if reality is wed,
with plans inside my neighbor's head,
the ruins will, by then, be rottened.

A thousand years from now what I have done, and do, may
be lost in memory and meaning.

But not for now, and not for you,
for now I'm filled with thoughts and feelings,
as real to life,
a thousand years from now,
or hence,
as any meaning.

3 Writing

3.1 Artistry

I close my eyes and listen.

Is there a poem there to be born?

I have fear there is not?

Little I can do.

What is an artist?

Nothing more than a listener, a vessel.

A vessel that moves what is heard to where it can be heard.

A vessel that moves what is seen to where it can be seen.

It comes from somewhere else.

Listening and being a vessel is artistry.

3.2 Finding Myself

I write

    not for love,

    and not for fun,

    and not for hopes of fame.

It is

    to fill the hole within myself

    with words that can explain.

Explain

    the inside to the out,

    the how I see and feel,

    the where I am and near,

    the what I want and fear.

I write to touch myself,

To tell me I am real.

3.3 Infant Messengers

If ink from pen
could come from me
to find its way upon a page,
and make with words
a masterpiece that could fire the flame
that burns inside the soul of all of us,
then words would work and I could feel complete,
but this can never be,
for words are infant messengers that cannot speak
what they are told to say.

4 Dreams & Fantasies

4.1 Speak to life with a Song

It might be nice to be a bird,
to spread my wings wide and jump from the bouncing limb
of a high tree.

To see the ground beneath,
and feel the air I push against to rise.

To sail high,
leisurely above the rabbits and cows and fences,
seeing them far below as moving specks.

And through clouds that leave a mist on my eye,
to put my head down,
and through the wind see everything draw closer.
Fighting the air with opened eyes,
then, using strength from exhilaration,
tilt, hold, and soar skyward.
Skyward to a point of calm, and a place to fly onward.

It might be nice to be a bird,
To own nothing but the wings

that can take you where you want to go.
To know the ground as a place to visit,

     and a tall tree as a place to rest and sleep.
To feel water roll down an outstretched neck,

     and to place twigs together for a home.
To talk to life,

     and speak to it with a song.

4.2   Finding and Living

I was alone, surrounded by a stern crowd.
Every critical, piercing eye stung deep within me.

The ill-fitting clothes I wore formed wrinkles on my soul,
for my mind was filled with the sour thoughts I knew others
had as they gazed at me.

The paused, trying words, I faintly spoke, crept from my
worried lips, with my already knowing they would fail me in
my desire to be accepted.

There was no friend who knew me, no refuge,
no place to rest and recover from my sorrows and loneliness.

My skin was sore. I prayed, and hoped, and wished I could
somehow be the things that others wanted me.

From my soreness, pain, anger, I, in desperation,
gave up on others, and decided to live what I believe.

Without pausing to care, or wonder how they wanted me to
be, I lived my life, not giving a damn if I was liked.

I was not after revenge. I was honest. I was kind. I was me.
And, I want you to know, I was liked,
and I hadn't even tried to be.

People spoke to me, smiled at me, came to me, respected me,
and I respected me, just because I lived my life and was what
I believed.

I stood alone with others always watching me.
I thought of what I couldn't do, and dreamed of things I
wanted to.

Then, I looked at things that I believe, and finally found the
nerve to leave the ways that others wanted me.

Now, I think of things I want to do,
and dream of things I'm going to.

And when I reach my final day,
I'll look back on my life and say,
I'm glad that now my life is through,
I did those things I wanted to.

4.3   Healing is what Nature Does

The shining sun and whispering hum
that flirts with grass and tree,
Announce with easy calm and subtle strength,
tranquilly to me,
That winter's gone and life goes on
and birds can fill the air,
And healing is what nature does
while I was standing there.

4.4 Sensing

I close my eyes and listen.

I hear "Un Poco" from a Spanish lesson months ago,

Someone's fan or air conditioner,

a floor buffer downstairs (it just went off),

crickets outside, and an occasional car, in that order.

Why, in that order, I don't know? Maybe someone could tell me. Maybe I could tell me if I thought about it for a while, but I don't want to.

Sometimes I think about things like that.

I close my eyes and what do I feel?

Sweat on my face,

The pen in my hand,

My back against the wall, and my hips and legs on the bed,

In that order.

If I had a pain of some kind I'm sure I would feel that first.

Sweat is a kind of pain, isn't it?

I'm not hot.

I close my eyes and mouth and find I can't taste the sandwich I had earlier today.

If I can taste anything it is the same taste I have in the morning after getting up and before I brush my teeth. I did take a nap this afternoon.

Maybe a little peanut butter.

With my eyes open, I see too many things to write down, so I won't worry about that.

Color is nice. I'm glad I'm not colorblind. They say black and white are the only two that are not colors, but to me chrome does not seem like a color. I guess it is a type of grey with reflective qualities.

I wonder if we can feel sleep.

Too bad we are not awake to know. "Un Poco" is gone now. I had to think to remember I had heard it. I don't want to write about smelling. It may be the heat.

4.5 Lie on a Lullaby

I want to fly,

lie on a lullaby,

close my eyes,

and let the world go by.

I want more than sight and sound

and touch and feel.

I want to be a part of something real.

The senses tell of things to me,

but all comes secondhandedly.

I want to flow and be and grow,

and know the parts of things there are to know.

I want to fly,

lie on a lullaby,

melt inside,

and ride, and ride, and ride, and ride.

4.6 Feelings are a Present Thing

Feelings are a present thing.

They sing their song alone.

They can be heard

But can they hear?

And do they go

The places they belong?

5 Friends & Family

5.1 A Friend

Amidst the myriad of swirls, crests and depths,

Where even the brightest lights can be refracted,

and questioned,

Where plethora obscures reality,

Where there is no place to stand securely,

Exists a point of understanding,

A re-unification with what is real,

A spirit in matching frequency,

Exists an undeniable connection,

a friend.

5.2 Remembering Love

When you're weak and feeling weary
And your dreams are things
You can't see coming true,
Step into a thought forgotten
Remembering a person
Who spoke of love to you.

While inside that special feeling,
Feeling what may long be past,
Think of how you own that feeling
And of how that feeling lasts.

5.3 Promises

If you speak to me friend, not of Promises,

And feel to me what you feel in you,

The day will be full and filling,

And the future untainted by views.

5.4 Father's 62nd Birthday

It is for you

who knows the hard of day

and long of work.

It is for you

who gives the fruits of work away.

It is for you

who cares for everyone,

both large and small.

It is for you

who I salute today.

That resting is full of rest.

That loving friends are friends who love.

That living is what wishing was.

And it is for you

That it should be this way.

5.5 It's been Over a Year

My brother gave me the temporary markers that marked our parents' graves.

They died two days apart, so they were buried in a single service.

It's been over a year now.

We sat across a table, and each thought, as brothers we were close, but closer because our mother wanted that.

We talked about our change, and how we change others because of them.

We saw generations and our own death.

We saw what is important in living.

We were thankful for our talk.

My sister sent me some cookies from my mother's old recipe.

I could taste more than the cookies.

The recipe called for raisins, or chocolate chips. She said mom usually used raisins.

Half the cookies had raisins, and the other half had chocolate chips.

That was really perfect.

The raisin cookies reminded me most of my mother. They were wonderful. I really enjoyed them.

The ones with chocolate chips tasted the best.

I know mom would have liked that I had both kinds.

5.6 The Old House

Over the spine of the ridge
will be the old house, with its
full length porch and two stories,
and the oak tree, still casting its shadow
where the swing hung.

The veranda rocker will be creaking its lullaby
and the two hands that pulled me from the creek
will be curled around those carved
lion's heads, I once thought should be white.

The dirt road will be powdered with
some of the same dust my bicycle threw,
dust that made those sideways stops
at the mailboxes, so pleasing.

There will be the sound of plates
being set on a wooden table, along with
glasses ready for tea, and some
large bowls with scalloped edges.
I broke one of those bowls and never told.

I can almost smell the scent
of boiling beans and potatoes
drifting out through the screen door
that always made me look when it slammed.

5.7 At the End of the Day

At the end of the day when the sun's gone away,
And the stars are clear in sight,
Whippoorwills display their call to sway
A lone wondering delight.

As the cricket sings and the firefly wings
Through most any summer night,
The cool air brings a peace to the things
That seemed so big in the light.

When the moon sinks low and the calm winds blow,
With the family tucked in tight,
It is nice to know what your feelings show,
Everything can be alright.

About the author

Gordon Emmerson was born near Springfield, Misssouri. He moved to Australia when he was 21 years of age. He lives near Melbourne.

Gordon developed Resource Personality Theory and Therapy and has developed techniques for working with many psychological conditions.

www.ingramcontent.com/pod-product-compliance
Lightning Source LLC
Chambersburg PA
CBHW081301040426
42452CB00014B/2595